The Science of Acne and Warts

The Itchy Truth About Skin

Written by
Alex Woolf

Franklin Watts®
An Imprint of Scholastic Inc.

Contents

Introduction

Your skin is your body's coat. It covers everything inside you. Muscles, bones, blood, organs—your skin keeps it all in place. It also keeps bad stuff out, like germs. Skin helps control your body's temperature and gives you the sensations of touch, heat, and cold.

Although it is extremely useful, skin can also be frustrating. It can itch, sting, bruise, form blisters, and flare up into rashes and spots. Some parts of your skin, like your feet and under your arms, can smell really bad, especially after exercise.

Skin can also be a positive thing. It is a part of our identity—of who we are. Our skin's color, its moles and birthmarks—its freckles, if we have them—are what make each of us unique. The scars we carry on our skin tell stories of past accidents and injuries.

We don't often think of our skin as an organ, but it is. In fact, it's the largest organ in the body. In this book we'll take a look at the fascinating truth about skin.

The Layers of the Skin

An average adult's skin is 21 square feet (2 square meters) if spread out flat. It weighs 9 pounds (4 kilograms) and contains around 11 miles (18 kilometers) of blood vessels.

Skin is made up of three layers. The epidermis is the outermost layer. It is usually about as thick as a sheet of paper, although it is thicker on the palms of the hands and soles of the feet. The middle layer is the dermis, which is 3 to 30 times thicker than the epidermis. The deepest and thickest layer is the subcutis. Its thickness varies depending on the part of the body it covers. Between them, these three layers help protect you, keep your body at the right temperature, and give you your sense of touch. Growing in and through the three layers are hairs, glands, nerves, and blood vessels.

Why doesn't that hurt?

Thick skin!

The epidermis contains lots of keratin, a tough, waterproof kind of protein that protects the skin.

6

Epidermis

The cells in the epidermis create melanin, which gives your skin its color. The surface of the epidermis is made of dead skin cells. At the bottom of the epidermis, new skin cells are continually forming. They replace the dead cells on the surface, which soon flake off.

Disgusting Data

Some of the dust in your home is actually dead skin. Every minute of the day, we lose 30,000 to 40,000 dead skin cells from the surface of our skin. That's almost 9 pounds (4 kg) of skin lost every year!

Dermis

The dermis contains nerve endings, which give you your sense of touch; blood vessels, bringing oxygen to your skin; oil glands, which produce sebum, your skin's natural oil; and sweat glands. The dermis also gives your skin its tough, stretchy quality.

Subcutis

The bottom layer of skin is made mostly of fat. It helps your body stay warm and absorb shocks. It also helps attach your skin to the tissues underneath it. This layer contains the roots of the hairs that grow out of your skin.

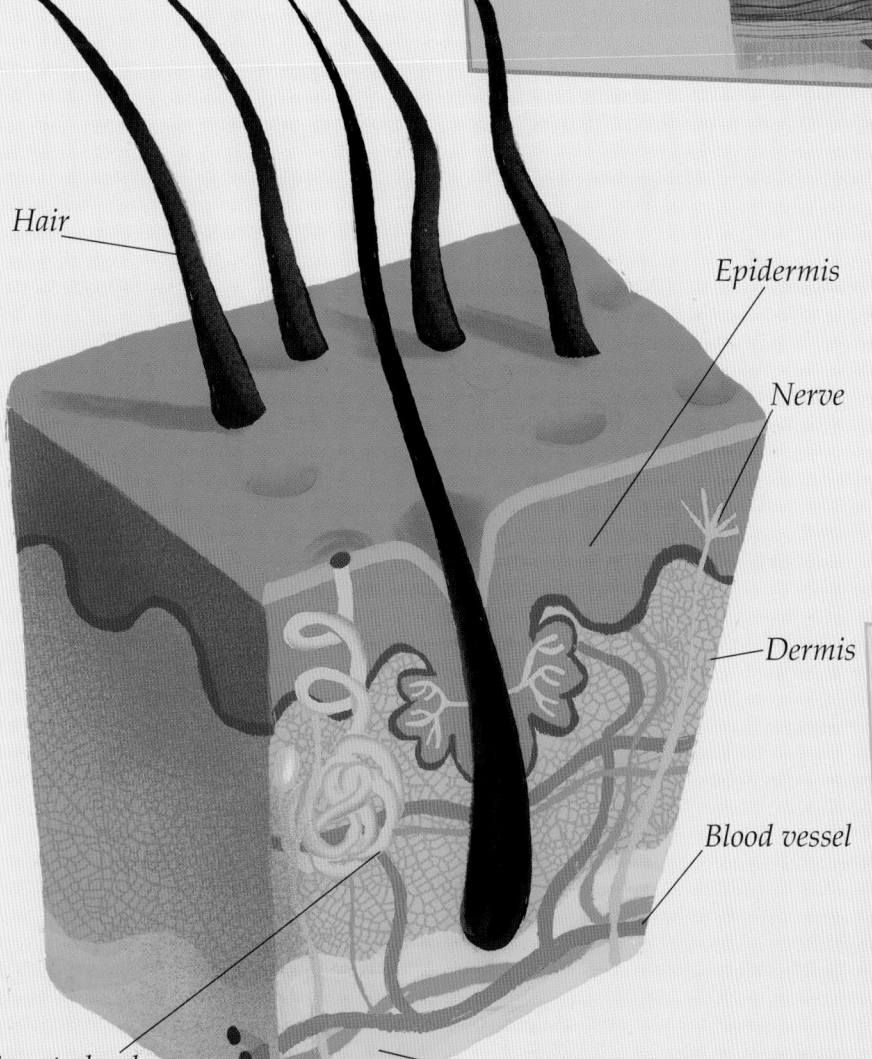

Hair

Epidermis

Nerve

Dermis

Blood vessel

Sweat gland

Subcutis

Sweat and Goosebumps

When your body feels cold, your skin forms goosebumps to make the hairs stand on end, trapping a layer of warm air next to the skin.

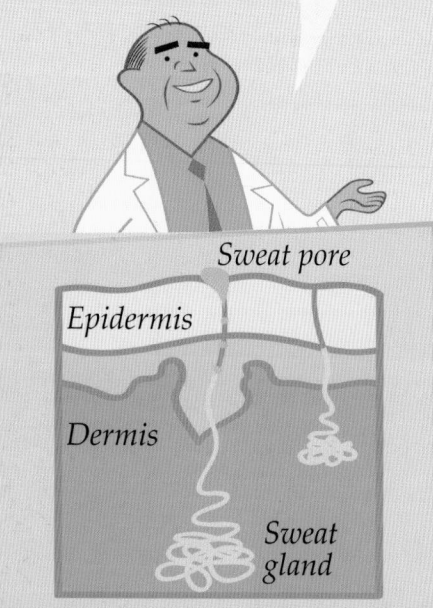

Sweat pore

Epidermis

Dermis

Sweat gland

What Is Sweat?

Sweat is mainly water, plus tiny amounts of other chemicals like ammonia, urea, salt, and sugar. Sweat oozes out onto the skin through tiny holes called pores. When the sweat meets the air, it evaporates (turns from liquid to vapor), which helps cool you down.

Your skin helps keep your body at the right temperature, which is about 98.6 degrees Fahrenheit (37 degrees Celsius). If you get too hot or too cold, your brain sends signals to your skin to take action. When you overheat, blood vessels carry warm blood from other parts of your body to the surface of your skin, which is why you sometimes get a red face when you run around. Sweat glands produce sweat to release body heat into the air and cool you down. When you get cold, your blood vessels get narrower, keeping the warm blood away from the skin's surface.

Did you fall in the pond again?

No, it's just sweat!

Why Does Sweat Smell?

Sweat doesn't actually smell at all—it's the bacteria that live on your skin mixing with the sweat that creates that bad smell. When you reach puberty, the glands in your armpits start making a different kind of sweat that can really smell. Regular washing and the use of deodorant helps.

Why Do Feet Smell?

There are more sweat glands in your feet than anywhere else in the body, and these glands produce lots of sweat. Bacteria living on the skin break this sweat down, releasing a cheesy smell in the process. Avoid smelly feet by washing your feet and changing your socks every day.

The skin releases up to 3 gallons (11 liters) of sweat a day in hot weather. If you exercise when it's hot, remember to drink plenty of water to replace lost fluids.

My feet are killing me!

They're killing me, too!

Fascinating Fact

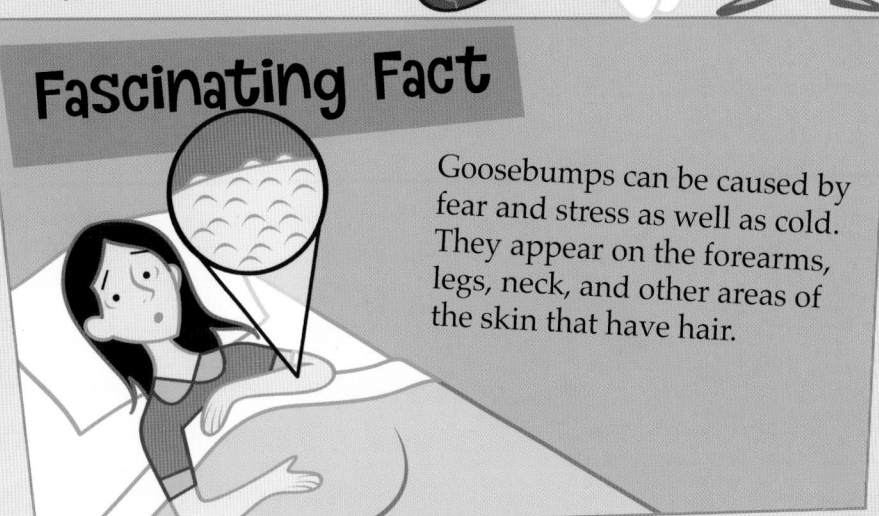

Goosebumps can be caused by fear and stress as well as cold. They appear on the forearms, legs, neck, and other areas of the skin that have hair.

What Is Acne?

Acne usually appears on the face, neck, shoulders, upper back, and chest.

Acne is a skin condition that causes pimples to appear. Teenagers often get acne because of increased levels of hormones during puberty. This causes the skin to produce more sebum. The pores become clogged with sebum and dead skin cells, forming a plug. Bacteria can get trapped inside the plug, causing a pimple—the start of acne. The mildest and most common pimples are whiteheads and blackheads. More serious are papules and pustules. The most severe forms of pimples are nodules and cysts.

How to Prevent Acne

To prevent the buildup of sebum, wash your face twice a day with mild soap and warm water. Don't scrub your face hard, because this can make things worse by irritating the pores.

Whitehead

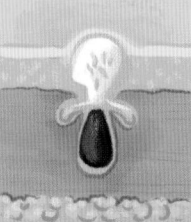

Clogged pore closes but bulges out from skin

Helpful Hint

You may be tempted to touch, squeeze, or pick at pimples. Don't! You can cause even more inflammation by opening them up. Picking at pimples can cause permanent scars.

Blackhead

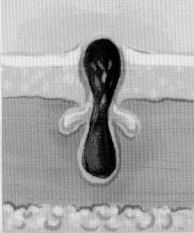

Clogged pore stays open so top surface darkens

Papule

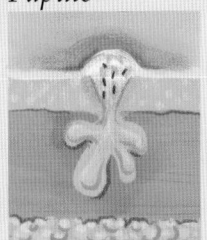

Wall of pore opens and lets in dirt, causing red bump

Pustule

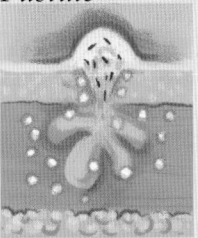

Papule with a pus-filled top

Cyst

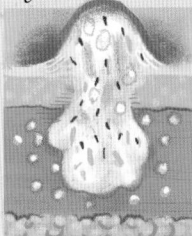

Nodule

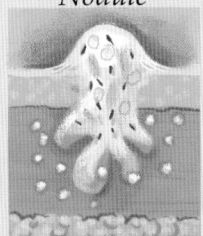

Severe acne can lead to scarring. This can be treated with laser resurfacing or dermabrasion, which wear down the damaged surface of the skin, allowing a new, smoother layer to replace it.

Large, painful, solid pimple

Deep, pus-filled pimple

How to Deal With Acne

There are creams and lotions available at the pharmacy to prevent and clear up acne. If you have persistent acne, see your doctor or dermatologist, who may treat it with creams or prescription medicines.

11

Blisters, Calluses, and Corns

If you wear shoes that don't fit properly, a blister can form on your feet within hours.

The skin on your feet and hands has to take a lot of punishment—especially if you do a lot of walking, or play sports or a musical instrument. Pressure from shoes on your feet, or a guitar string on your fingers, or a baseball bat against your hands can end up damaging your skin. The three main forms this damage can take are blisters, calluses, and corns. A blister is an area of raised skin with clear liquid inside. It can form very quickly on hands and feet due to rubbing and pressure on a particular spot.

Thick Skin

A callus is an area of thick skin. Unlike blisters, calluses take a long time to form, and they happen in areas where there is a lot of repeated rubbing over a lengthy period. The skin gradually hardens and thickens, forming a tough, yellowish surface.

What Are Calluses?

Calluses on the hands can be a form of protection. They allow gymnasts and guitarists to perform without hurting themselves. But calluses on the underside of the feet, caused by tight or high-heeled shoes, for example, can be painful because you have to step on them repeatedly.

Hey! Great calluses!

See what you get when you put in the effort?

Blisters!

Helpful Hint

Soak calluses in warm, soapy water and then rub with a pumice stone to get rid of the dead skin. For corns, you can buy special doughnut-shaped pads. The corn fits into the hole in the middle to relieve the pain and pressure.

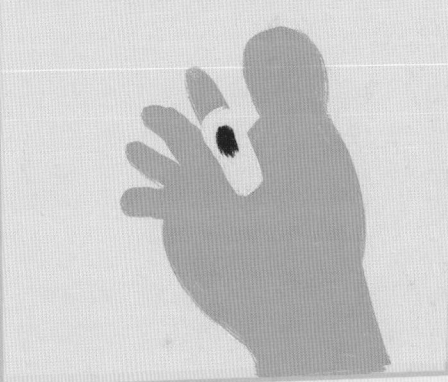

The thickest skin is found on the soles of your feet and it's 0.05 of an inch (1.3 millimeters) thick. The thinnest skin is found on your eyelids—it's just 0.019 of an inch (0.5 mm) thick.

Corns

A corn is a buildup of hard skin on the top of or in between toes. It usually appears as a soft yellow ring of skin around a hard, gray center. Corns usually develop from wearing shoes that are tight in the toe area, causing rubbing and friction.

13

Cuts, Scars, and Bruises

Scars occur because the body produces special proteins called collagen fibers to mend damaged skin. This forms scar tissue, which looks and feels different from normal skin.

Scar tissue does not contain hair follicles, sweat glands, or oil glands. That's why it looks smoother than undamaged skin and can become itchy.

If you lead an active life, chances are that sooner or later you'll have an accident and maybe cut or bruise yourself. Sometimes the cut might heal and disappear. Other times it may leave a scar. A scar is a pale pink, brown, or silvery patch of skin. Sometimes you may receive a knock or a blow that doesn't damage the surface of the skin, but breaks the blood vessels beneath. This is a bruise. The blood leaks out of the blood vessels and spreads out inside the skin, causing a dark mark. It often looks purple-blue to start with. After a few days, it fades to a yellow-green before eventually disappearing.

I got this fighting a tiger!

I got this falling out of bed!

14

What Is a Clot?

When you cut yourself, platelets in your blood cause the blood to clot. The clot hardens to form a scab, which protects the wound while new skin is made and blood vessels are repaired. When the cut is healed, the scab falls off.

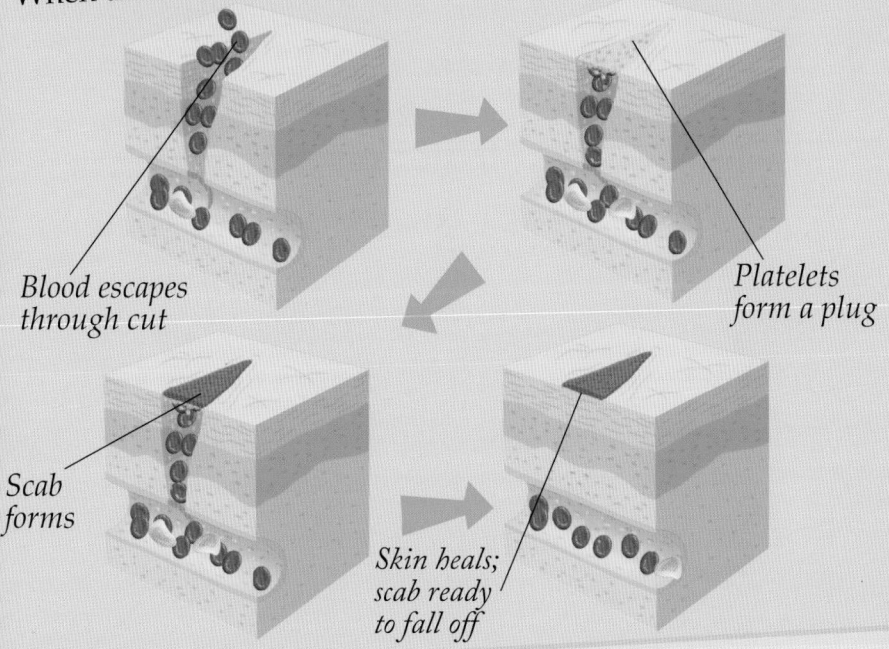

Blood escapes through cut

Platelets form a plug

Scab forms

Skin heals; scab ready to fall off

Stretch Marks

Sometimes people can get scars called stretch marks when their skin is forced to stretch more than it can expand. This can happen to women during pregnancy and to teenagers during growth spurts.

What's wrong, Elastic Man?

I've got stretch marks!

Stitches

If a wound is very long or deep, you may need stitches. The doctor will numb the skin with an anesthetic, then sew the edges of the wound together with a small needle and special thread. Once the wound has healed, the doctor takes the stitches out. Some stitches dissolve over time and don't need to be removed.

Fascinating Fact

Sometimes, instead of stitches, the doctor will use a special kind of glue that closes up the wound to allow the skin to heal. The glue dissolves over time.

15

Fungal Infections and Warts

There are between 1.5 and 5 million species of fungi. Every cubic meter of air contains over 10,000 fungal spores (reproductive cells).

I think it may be a fungal infection.

When you hear the word *fungus*, you might think of mushrooms. But fungi take many different forms. One type of fungus likes to live on skin, where it feeds on keratin (a protein that makes up the dead, outer layer of the epidermis, as well as our hair and nails). Fungi love warm, damp places, such as between the toes. Common fungal infections include athlete's foot and ringworm. Warts are small, hard lumps that appear on the skin. They are caused by a virus called the human papillomavirus (HPV). The virus gets into the skin through tiny cuts.

After a fungal infection starts, it can take weeks or even months for a wart to appear. This is called the incubation period.

Athlete's Foot and Ringworm

Athlete's foot makes the skin between your toes dry, red, cracked, flaky, and itchy. You can catch it walking barefoot on damp floors, or by sharing towels. Ringworm is a fungal infection of the hair, nails, or skin. When it's on the skin, it forms a red, ring-shaped rash.

I'm not sure how I got athlete's foot!

Plantar Warts

Warts may be ugly to look at, but they're mostly painless. One exception is plantar warts, or verrucas. These are warts that develop on the soles of the feet. As a result, they tend to hurt—it feels like you're walking on a small pebble.

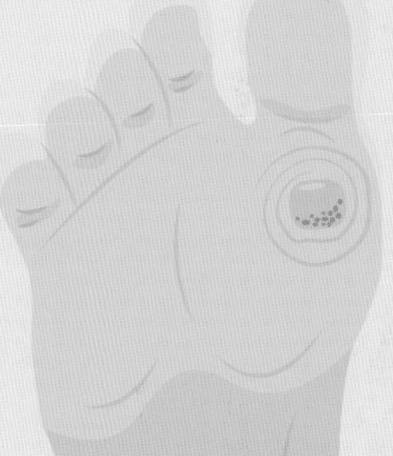

Warts

A wart is a lump of keratin. Warts are commonly caught in places where people walk around in bare feet, such as public swimming pools, communal showers, and gyms.

I'm looking for warts!

??

Helpful Hint

To prevent athlete's foot:
• Wash your feet every day and dry them thoroughly.
• Wear sandals or flip-flops in public showers, changing rooms, and swimming pools.
• Wear clean socks.
• Use a medicated powder on your feet to help reduce sweating.

Eczema

Eczema is a common kind of rash that makes your skin dry and itchy. It's an allergic reaction to things like soaps, detergents, and certain fabrics. Scratching makes it worse. Eczema is common among children but can affect people at any age.

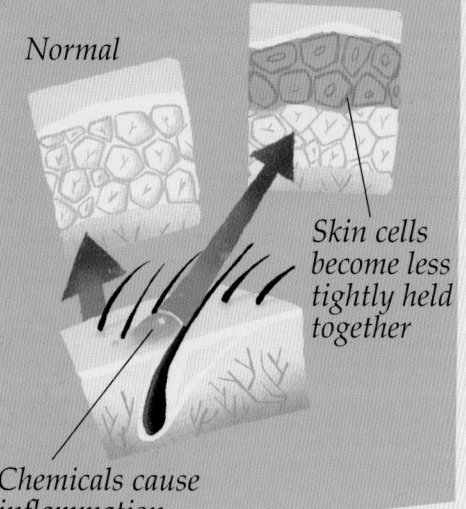

Normal

Eczema

Skin cells become less tightly held together

Chemicals cause inflammation

If you have eczema, avoid substances your skin is sensitive to.

Skin Rashes

A skin rash is an area of skin that has become red and inflamed. The skin might become bumpy, dry, cracked, blistered, or swollen. It might feel itchy or sore. Skin rashes have many causes. Some, such as chicken pox, shingles, measles, and impetigo, are caused by a virus or bacteria. Others, like eczema, hives, and contact dermatitis, are caused by allergic reactions to certain foods or other substances. Sometimes you can get a rash from contact with plants such as poison ivy or stinging nettles. One rash, intertrigo, occurs in folds of skin, such as armpits and under belly folds.

Why are you scratching yourself?

No one else knows where I itch!

Psoriasis

This condition causes red, flaky patches of skin covered with silvery scales, usually on the elbows, knees, scalp, and lower back. It's caused by increased production of skin cells. Skin cells are normally replaced every 3 to 4 weeks; with psoriasis, they are replaced every 3 to 7 days.

Fascinating Fact

Dermographism is a type of hives. If you have this condition, you can write words or draw patterns on your skin with your finger. A rash appears where you touched the skin, about 15 minutes later. The rash goes away after 15 to 30 minutes.

Some people get skin rashes from contact with everyday substances. These include leather (due to chemicals used in the tanning process), coins (a reaction to nickel), and prolonged contact with water.

Shingles

Shingles is caused by the same virus responsible for chicken pox. It causes a painful rash that develops into itchy blisters. It always appears on one area of the body and lasts 2 to 4 weeks.

Freckles, Moles, and Birthmarks

Moles

Moles are small brownish spots on the skin made up of melanocytes. They can be flat or raised, and some have hair growing from them. Most moles are harmless, though you can have them removed if you find them unsightly or a nuisance.

In rare cases, a mole can turn into a melanoma, a dangerous form of skin cancer. A melanoma usually appears as a dark, fast-growing spot.

Many of us have marks or patches on our skin that aren't harmful, they're just part of who we are. Freckles, for example, are small, light-brown spots. They are skin cells that contain a pigment called melanin, which makes the skin darker. Melanin helps protect the skin from the sun's harmful rays. It's produced by skin cells called melanocytes. The sun's rays cause melanocytes to make more melanin, which causes freckles to appear or get darker.

I wish I had your freckles.

Sorry, they're not transferable!

Types of Birthmarks

Salmon patches

Strawberry marks

Port-wine stains

Café-au-lait spots

Birthmarks

Birthmarks get their name because we're born with them, or they appear soon after birth. The main kinds are vascular birthmarks (usually pink, red, or purple) caused by clusters of blood vessels in or under the skin; and pigmented birthmarks (usually brown) caused by clusters of pigment cells.

He has a birthmark!

It's beautiful!

Helpful Hint

To avoid getting a melanoma, be careful in the sun, because overexposure to the sun's harmful ultraviolet (UV) rays increases your chances of developing one.

Tanning

The sun's rays contain two types of UV radiation: UVA and UVB. UVA rays penetrate to the lower epidermis, triggering the melanocytes to produce more melanin, causing the skin to tan. UVB rays burn the skin's surface, causing sunburn.

Remember to put on sunscreen, or you may turn into bacon!

Skin Color

Human skin comes in many different colors, from pale to dark. Our skin color is determined by where our ancestors lived. People whose roots lie in warmer, tropical parts of the world tend to have darker skin than those from colder climates. Darker skin gave protection from the sun's ultraviolet (UV) radiation. Our skin color depends on the amount of the pigment melanin that our melanocytes produce. Small amounts of melanin result in light skin, while large amounts produce dark skin. Everyone has a similar amount of melanocytes (they make up around 7 percent of our skin cells), but in darker-skinned people, they produce more melanin.

The extra melanin produced when you tan protects the skin from burning, but it cannot protect against skin cancer and other problems.

Around 1 in 110,000 people have albinism, which means they don't produce melanin. They have very pale skin and white hair.

Helpful Hint

Protect your skin from the sun's UV rays, especially if you have fair skin. Use sunscreen with an SPF (sun protection factor) of at least 15; wear a wide-brimmed hat, sunglasses, and suitable clothing; sit in the shade during the hottest part of the day.

Vitamin D

People whose ancestors came from cooler climates tend to have lighter skin tones to allow more sunlight to penetrate the skin to help produce vitamin D, which the body needs. However, native peoples from Alaska and Canada had somewhat darker skin because of their Asian ancestry. And because their diet was heavy in vitamin D, their skin didn't lighten over time in order to absorb it.

Vitiligo

Vitiligo is a loss of skin pigment that causes white spots or patches to appear on the skin. The melanocytes stop producing melanin. No one knows why this happens, but it isn't harmful or infectious. Usually it happens in areas of skin exposed to the sun, or skin that has folds, like elbows or knees.

Melanin is also responsible for eye color. Little melanin gives blue eyes; some melanin gives green or light brown eyes; lots of melanin gives dark brown eyes.

23

Bites and Stings

Bee Stings

Honeybees' stingers consist of barbed prongs that dig into your skin. Between the prongs runs a hollow tube through which the venom is injected. Because they are barbed, the prongs remain stuck in the skin, pulling out part of the bee's abdomen when it flies away. As a result, the bee dies.

Anyone who's spent time outdoors in the summer has probably been bitten or stung by an insect. Bugs that bite include mosquitoes, fleas, spiders, mites, sandflies, and ticks. They make a hole in your skin to feed on your blood. When they bite, they release saliva. The saliva contains a chemical that stops your blood from clotting. Your body responds to this by releasing chemicals called histamines, which make your skin red, swollen, and itchy. Insects such as bees, wasps, and hornets sting as a means of defense by injecting venom into your skin. The venom attacks nerve cells, causing you pain.

This will hurt me more than it hurts you!

Stings get red and swollen because the body releases histamines in response to the venom.

Pick on someone your own size!

Mosquito Bites

The mouthparts of a mosquito are usually hidden inside a sheath called the labium. When a mosquito lands on you, the labium bends back, and needlelike mouthparts emerge to pierce your skin, while hollow mouthparts inject saliva and suck up your blood.

I love biting elbows.

I'm more of an ankle girl.

If you're bitten by an insect, wash the affected area with soap and water; place a cold, wet cloth over the area to reduce swelling; and buy antihistamine medicine for pain and itching.

Anaphylaxis

For some people, bites and stings can trigger a major allergic reaction called anaphylaxis. This can include skin rashes, swollen eyes or mouth, lightheadedness, pain, nausea, wheezing, and unconsciousness. People with anaphylaxis should be injected with epinephrine (adrenaline) as soon as possible.

Helpful Hint

• Use insect repellant when outdoors during the summer.
• Don't panic or wave your arms around when encountering bees and wasps. Back away slowly. But if attacked, run away and find shelter.
• If traveling to Africa, Asia, or South America, remember to get vaccinated against malaria and other diseases spread by insect bites.

Animal Skin

The Bornean flat-headed frog has no lungs. It gets all its oxygen through its skin.

Throughout the natural world, there are examples of animals that use their skin in extraordinary ways. Skin is used for camouflage, self-defense, breathing, drinking, and keeping cool. Crocodiles use their skin for hunting. They have special receptors in the skin of their faces that are more sensitive than human fingertips. They are able to feel the faintest ripples in the water, enabling them to locate and bite their prey. The sun bear of Southeast Asia has very loose neck skin. This allows it to turn around and bite animals that attack it from behind.

Go on! Attack me from behind, I dare you!

Regenerating Skin

The African spiny mouse has very tender, easily tearable skin. This is actually a form of defense: If a predator catches it, the mouse's skin will peel right off. Amazingly, the mouse then regenerates new skin, complete with hair follicles and sweat glands, in just a few days.

Run away if you want to save your skin!

I think not.

The Thickest Skin

The sperm whale has the thickest skin in the world. It can be up to 13.7 inches (35 centimeters) thick! It probably needs this kind of protection because it preys on giant squid, which have razor-studded tentacles.

> Insult me all you like, I'm very thick skinned!

Poison dart frogs from South America keep poison in glands beneath their skin as a defense against predators. One species, the golden poison frog, has enough poison in its skin to kill ten human adults!

Can You Believe It?

The thorny devil, a lizard from the Australian desert, actually drinks with its feet. Its foot skin is full of microscopic cracks that suck up water in a process called capillary action.

Skin Made of Eyes

Octopuses and cuttlefish can change their skin color to match their surroundings, in order to evade predators. How do they do it, considering they are color-blind? They actually have light-sensing cells in their skin that can match the patterns and colors around them.

As We Get Older

Doctors believe that regular exercise and cutting down on carbohydrates (for example, bread and pasta) can help reduce the chance of early wrinkles.

Why Do We Get Wrinkles?

When you are young, your dermis is stretchy because it contains elastin and collagen. Over time, the dermis loses these proteins. The skin gets thinner, and the fat in the subcutis that gives skin its plumpness starts to disappear. As a result, the skin sags and wrinkles form.

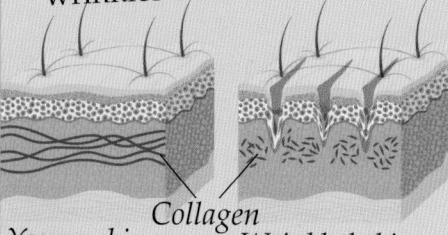

Young skin   *Collagen*   *Wrinkled skin*

As people age, their skin becomes wrinkled. The epidermis gets thinner and the number of melanocytes decreases, making the skin paler and more translucent. Large brown spots appear in sun-exposed areas. The blood vessels in the dermis become more fragile, leading to frequent bruising. The sebaceous glands produce less oil, making skin drier. The subcutis (fat layer) gets thinner, so elderly people are less insulated from the cold and from injury. The sweat glands produce less sweat, making it harder to keep cool in hot weather.

My skin isn't wrinkled, it's just a loose fit!

Breathing Causes Wrinkles

Each time you take a breath, oxygen molecules known as free radicals attack the cells in your body that produce collagen. Over a long period of time, this leads to wrinkles. Certain foods, including tomatoes, broccoli, radishes, and oily fish, prevent the damage caused by free radicals.

Getting early wrinkles can also be due to your genes—some families are more prone to wrinkles than others.

When Do We Get Wrinkles?

The first wrinkles often appear around the eyes ("crow's feet"). They can come at any age, from the late twenties onward. It depends partly on your lifestyle—people who spend a lot of time in the sun are more likely to get wrinkles earlier.

Don't worry, it's perfectly normal to get crow's feet!

Helpful Hints

To avoid early wrinkles:
- Don't spend too much time in the sun, especially in the middle of the day.
- Don't go to the tanning salon. The UV light there is just as damaging as the sun's.
- Don't smoke. Smoking dries the skin and causes early wrinkles.
- Drink lots of water.
- Use moisturizer on dry skin.

Glossary

Allergic reaction A damaging response by the body to a substance.

Anesthetic A substance that makes someone insensitive to pain.

Bacteria Microscopic organisms that may cause disease.

Blister A small bubble on the skin that may be caused by friction or burning.

Café-au-lait spots Coffee-colored birthmarks.

Cancer A disease caused by the uncontrolled growth of cells in a part of the body.

Carbohydrate Substances found in foods such as potatoes and pasta that give the body energy.

Clotting (of blood) Turning thicker and more sticky. This happens to blood when it is exposed to air, for example, when you get a cut.

Contact dermatitis A type of eczema caused by contact with a particular substance.

Dermatologist A doctor who deals with skin disorders.

Dermis The thick layer of skin below the epidermis, containing blood vessels, nerve endings, sweat glands, and hair follicles.

Epidermis The outer layer of skin. It has a surface of dead skin cells, and new, forming skin cells at its base.

Fungal infection An infection caused by a fungus that feeds on living matter.

Gene A sequence of chemicals inside our cells. They are passed on by parent to child and determine things like eye and skin color.

Gland An organ in the body that produces particular chemical substances that the body uses or releases.

Hair follicle A hollow area in the skin that surrounds the root of a hair.

Histamine A chemical released by the body during an allergic reaction.

Hormones Chemicals made by glands in the body that affect the way we grow and develop.

Impetigo An infection that causes pustules and yellow crusty sores on the skin.

Keratin A fiber-like protein that is the main substance in hair.

Melanin A dark brown to black pigment found in skin, hair, and the irises of eyes.

Melanocyte A melanin-producing skin cell.

Pigment A substance that gives color to something.

Platelet A small, disc-shaped cell fragment found in the blood.

Pore A tiny opening in the skin through which sweat can escape.

Port-wine stains Flat red or purple birthmarks, often on the face, chest, or back. They tend to be permanent.

Protein A type of chemical essential to all living organisms.

Salmon patches Flat red or pink patches that appear on a baby's eyelids, neck, or forehead; they disappear by around age four.

Sebaceous gland A small gland in the skin that discharges sebum into the hair follicles to lubricate the skin and hair.

Sebum An oily substance secreted by the sebaceous gland.

Strawberry marks Raised red birthmarks that can appear anywhere; they disappear at around age seven.

Subcutis Also known as the subcutaneous layer, this is the deepest layer of the skin, and is used mainly for fat storage.

Sweat gland A small gland in the dermis that discharges sweat.

Vaccinated Treated with a vaccine, a substance that gives immunity to a disease.

Vascular Relating to blood vessels.

Index